All Cat Wants for Christmas

Cats Talk to Santa

Lizz Brady

Illustrations by Alisa Harris

MJF BOOKS
New York

Published by MJF Books
Fine Communications
322 Eighth Avenue
New York, NY 10001

All Cat Wants for Christmas
LC Control Number: 2015909750
ISBN 978-1-60671-310-5

Printed in the United States of America.

Designed by Lisa Chovnick
Illustrations by Alisa Harris

MJF Books and the MJF colophon are trademarks
of Fine Creative Media, Inc.

QF   10   9   8   7   6   5   4   3   2

For Curly, Mom, Dad, D. J., Mary Alice
. . . and even Dagi

DEAR SANTA,

Thank you again for the kitty condo you got me last Christmas. I'm sure it wasn't cheap. It's so tall and it takes up so much space! I can see why you thought I'd be impressed.

But Santa: Did you know how GREAT the box that it came in was? I couldn't stay out of that thing! My human couldn't believe it either.

"Typical," she muttered, and then a few days later she accidentally put the box out with the recycling. Can you save us some confusion this Christmas by just bringing me an empty box? I can't wait to get busy lying in it all day!

Love,
Smoky

Hɪ Sᴀɴᴛᴀ,

Do you happen to have the *other*, better brand of cat litter in your bag of presents? For my human's sake, I really hope so!

Farah

DEAR SANTA,

If my humans don't want me to make that "face," maybe they should change their socks more often. Breath mints would also make a great stocking stuffer. I'm not criticizing—I'm just being a good friend.

Besides, who doesn't love getting socks for Christmas?

Sincerely,
Poppy

DEAR SANTA,

Becoming an Internet sensation is *much* harder than it looks. I have busted out all of the adorable tricks in my arsenal, but it is hard work.

Will you bring me more page views this Christmas? Those endorsement deals and convention appearances aren't going to book themselves!

Thanks,
Winnie

DEAR SANTA,

I have thought long and hard about what food
item I most want you to bring me this Christmas—
it's string cheese! Oh, man, do I love a good
stick of string cheese.

Full disclosure: I don't really like the taste of
string cheese. But it's very important that I have
the string cheese in front of me to sniff and remind
myself that, no, I actually don't like string cheese.
Just trust the process, Santa.

Your pal,
Pancakes

DEAR SANTA,

How many mirrors would you say are enough for one house? I think our place could use fifteen to twenty more, at a minimum. Some softer lighting would also be fabulous.

Yours,
Claudio

DEAR SANTA,

CAT BUTTS EXIST.

That's exactly what I'd like the sampler to say. Red block letters are preferable.

I'm getting pretty fed up with the sour faces and "ewwws" around here when I'm just trying to get comfortable on top of the humans. Is it a crime to face the other direction once in a while? Can I know what my tail is doing 24-7?

Best,
Duncan

DEAR SANTA,

Maybe I'm imagining things, but these days the dog seems to be much tenser and tightly wound. Instead of centering himself and stopping to smell the roses (peeing on them doesn't count), it's all "bark, bark, bark" and "go, go, go!" Seeing him under so much stress breaks my heart.

Could you bring me brochures for some ashrams in India where he could stay for a while to better align his chakras? I'm sure once my humans read them they will be persuaded to let him stay there however many months (or years) it takes for him to achieve a higher plane of consciousness.

Namaste,
Callie

Dear Santa,

It seems my humans are struggling with the concept of "sharing."

I didn't *want* to ask you for a crib this Christmas, but since they keep tossing me out of the baby's, I have no choice but to request my own.

Thanks,
Ava

Hi Santa,

Feel free to use our bathroom on your way out. I know you have a long night of deliveries ahead of you. It's no trouble at all, honest!

I should probably mention that we have an "open door" policy in this house concerning the bathroom. You don't have to leave the door wide open (that would be weird), a sliver will do.

I just want to nudge my way in for some friendly conversation and to collect my Christmas wish from you: some extra ear scratches while I have your undivided attention!

Paw Simon

Hi Santa,

Nothing good ever happens when the cat carrier is brought down from the attic. I will give you my weight in tuna to make that thing disappear. PERMANENTLY.

Abe

DEAR SANTA,

My human keeps closing the lid on the piano! How am I supposed to keep up with my practicing? Is she trying to tell me that I'm no good at it and that I should quit?

Talk about passive-aggressive. Please bring me a drum set.

Thank you,
Oreo

Dear Santa,

For Christmas this year I would like an assortment of bags to dive into from across the room. Paper, plastic, large, or small—I'm not picky, but a nice cross section is preferable. They will aid in my ongoing study: "What's Noisiest?"

My human has callously pulled funding for this research, so between the hours of 1:00 and 4:00 a.m. I can only experiment with whatever bags she forgets to pick up off the floor. Isn't that around the time you usually drop by? If so, I look forward to working with you!

Yours,
Owen

Hi Santa,

Oh, great, new luggage! I've wanted a new suitcase for ages.

Wait, before you go, aren't you going to open it so I can sleep inside? That *is* why suitcases exist, correct?

                                                    Candy

Dear Santa,

All I want this Christmas is a laptop screen I can head-butt in peace.

                                                    Yours,
                                                    Miss Marbles

DEAR SANTA,

This Christmas you can have the cookies my humans leave out for you, but I would appreciate it if you left the milk for me.

If you're really thirsty, I don't mind some friendly gambling. We can race around the tree or pull names out of your cap if you want; but no rock-paper-scissors—I'm terrible at that game.

Best,
Jack

Dear Santa,

There seems to be some confusion around here regarding belly rubs. For Christmas, could you bring me an "OPEN/CLOSED FOR BUSINESS" sign so I can wear it around my neck?

I think my humans will be grateful to have this info, and they will definitely save a lot of money on hydrogen peroxide.

Sincerely,
Coconut

DEAR SANTA,

I don't like the bugs with all of the legs either! Why do my humans expect me to hunt those? Is that in my cat contract, and are you also a lawyer?

If the answer is "yes," please amend that language, because NO WAY.

Best,
Frances Bacon

DEAR SANTA,

For Christmas I guess you can get me that scratching post my humans keep talking about.

I'm not sure why they yell and get so excited about a dumb piece of carpet, but I'll use it once or twice while they are in the room. After they leave, I will resume using the perfectly good sofa arm.

Thanks,
Casey

Dear Santa,

No matter what anyone tells you, this Christmas I do *not* want a cheeseburger.

I don't know why so many other cats love them, but that's their business.

Sincerely,
Billie

Dear Santa,

Christmas this year is coming not a moment too soon. Our household desperately needs a new bathroom sink. The faucet we have now keeps shutting off in front of me without warning, ending my stream of precious, life-giving water.

Alarmingly, my humans don't see the problem. They insist that a bowl of FLAT, NON-MOVING water is the same thing. As we both know, Santa, NOT THE SAME.

Once they see a working sink, I'm sure they'll wonder how we ever lived with the broken one for so long. It's a good thing they have me around.

Thank you,
Dagi

DEAR SANTA,

Eek! Can you bring me a root touch-up kit for my whiskers? I can barely keep on top of all these whites. Getting old is a drag.

Love,
Anna

P. S. "Sumptuous Sable" is my go-to.

Dear Santa,

A "cat café" that's also teeming with gawking, grabby humans is very misleading.

If you could take me to a café operated and patronized solely by cats, it would save me from having to write a lot of negative Yelp reviews.

Thank you,
Holly

Dear Santa,

Please don't be offended if I'm fast asleep when you get to the house. My days are very long and draining.

However, if I'm doing bicycle kicks in my sleep, could you wake me up? Bad dreams are the worst!

You friend,
Princess

Dear Santa,

Pancakes here again—hi!

I know in my last letter I said the one food item I most want for Christmas is string cheese, but it just dawned on me: Could you throw in some shrimp tails?

And if it's not too much trouble, can you save me some time by scattering the shrimp tails around the house? Oh, you know, wherever. Under the couch cushions, behind the radiator, in a clog—I trust your judgment. I'll get around to eating most of them by next Christmas.

Thanks again,
Pancakes

Hi Santa,

As you can see, the humans decided—yet again—
to express their gratitude toward you with milk and
cookies. But this year I was determined to think
outside the box.

That's why your present is under an
overturned bowl on the porch. I wanted to give it
to you myself, but when the humans saw it in my
mouth they started screeching and flailing.

Anyway, your present has probably stopped
moving by now, but you should probably pick the
bowl up very carefully just in case.

Merry Christmas!
Peppermint

DEAR SANTA,

Just confirming—has catnip been legalized in my state? If so, I will take as much as you can carry!

Love,
Sam

HI SANTA,

How would you like Mrs. Claus to smother YOU in a towel to "trim your nails?" Put those shiny new clippers back in the bag, pronto, or the fancy suit turns to shreds.

Tallulah

Dᴇᴀʀ Sᴀɴᴛᴀ,

There *is* a downside to the earth revolving around me: I'm not getting enough sunlight. I try to sit in a patch whenever I can find one, but it still goes away sometimes. Dark and cloudy days are the pits.

May I have a sunlamp? There has not been as much media attention paid to KSAD (Kitty Seasonal Affective Disorder), but I assure you: it's a thing.

Yours,
Lars

Dear Santa,

A great stocking stuffer this Christmas would be more AA batteries. I have found AA is the optimal size of battery for me to swipe across the floor and under the furniture at night when my toys start to bore me.

Just so you know, C- and D-size are much too big for my delicate paws, and AAA does not produce the level of oomph I'm looking for in swatting power. AA is just right. I guess you could call me the Goldilocks of batteries.

Sincerely,
Sheva

DEAR SANTA,

This Christmas I would like a "dresser" of my own. My human has one with drawers that turn into very comfy beds. When she catches me sleeping in them she tells me how cute I am (well, duh) and sometimes even takes my picture.

Except five minutes later I am rudely picked up and told I do not belong there before being plopped on the floor.

I can't take these mixed signals any longer—time for my own set of beds.

Yours,
Nina

Dear Santa,

For Christmas, I would like the loudest alarm clock you have—the louder the better.

My human is hard of hearing. Every morning I considerately tell her it is time to get up—a whole hour before her stupid alarm rings—but she ignores me, and then the alarm, and then me again.

Do they make any clocks attached to air horns? How about megaphones?

Your friend,
Quincy

Dear Santa,

The wet food! No, wait . . . the dry food. Actually, the wet food! No, no, definitely the dry food.

Please bring the dry food, but you'd better have the wet food on hand just in case. I like to keep my options open.

Best,
Muta

Dear Santa,

Merry Christmas! Will you cook me some spaghetti when you visit? My humans are hogging all of the cooked noodles.

Why wouldn't I also like noodles—because I'm a cat? That's a very species-ist assumption on their part.

Sincerely,
Frank

Dear Santa,

Yes, dental health is extremely important, especially for cats, blah blah blah—but please don't be "that guy."

Toothbrushes are never on Christmas lists for a reason. Cat treats, on the other hand . . .

Thanks,
Camille

Dear Santa,

For Christmas I would like my human's old box spring back. You and the reindeer might have to visit a lot of dumps before you find it, but you will recognize it by all of the giant holes carefully ripped through its bottom.

That box spring was my canvas, Santa! I spent ten years making those holes. Would you toss a Jackson Pollock in the landfill? Of course not!

Anyway, I'm sure if you bring it back to our house I can convince my human to call Christie's and have it appraised as the masterpiece it is.

Your friend,
Curly

HI SANTA,

Oof. Please watch where you step as you make your way around the Christmas tree. I ate dinner too fast again. I'm sorry!

Fidget

HI SANTA,

Yargh! All I want for Christmas is to finally WIN a staring contest!

Rusty

DEAR SANTA,

Every January 1 I tell myself, "Okay, Mitzy, this is your year—new year, new you! You don't need to eat all of the houseplants to feel fulfilled. You don't need to disappoint the humans with your lack of self-control. Channel those obsessive thoughts into something productive—sign up for Pilates! Start a scrapbook!" And still, every Christmas I'm right back to square one.

Enclosed is a list of all the plants that need replacing. I'll try harder next year. Sigh.

Your friend,
Mitzy

Dear Santa,

My Christmas wish is to befriend more humans who are allergic to cats. I love a good challenge!

Those spoilsports will come around. I mean, fine, so they're covered in hives—but how can they resist this face?

Your friend,
Mulder

DEAR SANTA,

What's the deal with the fish show? So far it's a total snooze fest. There seems to be no plot, no love triangles, and not even any dialogue. The fish just swim around in circles all day.

If you can't figure out how to turn it off, can you at least bring them a new castmate for Christmas? A piranha or a squid would definitely spice things up.

Thank you,
Steve

Hi Santa,

I've nudged a lot of faces in my time, so I don't say this to just anyone: Your face is one of the MOST nudge-able I've ever laid eyes on. It's in the top ten for sure.

Will you do my whiskers and cold nose the honor?

Tuck

DEAR SANTA,

The dog has been in quite a rut lately. Every day he walks the same routes, sniffs the same butts, squeaks the same toys—not to mention the broken record of "arf arf arfs." Wouldn't it be great for him to expand his worldview and maybe even pick up a new language?

I think we both know the solution . . . a foreign exchange program! I hear Siberia is lovely this time of year. If by next Christmas he isn't ready to come back, that's okay. I want to make sure he's completely immersed in his new culture.

Your friend,
Ollie

P.S. We don't need a Siberian husky to come live with us in exchange; I'm sure we'll learn just as much from a Siberian hamster.

DEAR SANTA,

For Christmas, can you please bring me a heavy-duty rain coat in my size?

That horrible spray bottle isn't going to be my arch nemesis much longer!

Sincerely,
Barney

Dear Santa,

No matter how much I shake the end of my tail, I can't get it to make noise. Will you bring me a rattlesnake's rattle?

This will make for a killer April Fools' Day joke in a few months.

Your pal,
Siggy

Dear Santa,

All I want this Christmas is a warm, freshly laundered pile of clothing.

I have white hair, so black-colored garments are the most comfortable for me to lounge on, but other dark items will do in a pinch.

Winter coats and suit jackets are especially wonderful for rolling on, and gym socks, which can be swiped under the bed. Oh, and bath towels, too—please don't forget the bath towels!

Yours truly,
Lucy

Dear Santa,

Is there a special mask I can wear to mute the sounds of my purring? I am very self-conscious about how loud it is.

Purring also renders my poker face completely useless. If the humans can tell when I'm happy, what's the point of being a cat?

Thanks,
Stormy

DEAR SANTA,

After you drop off my presents, could you swing by my human's bedroom on your way out and shave her head? If you could also leave her the following note, I'd be delighted:

"So you won't get too hot this summer—HA!"

That'll fix her wagon!

Okay, fine . . . maybe just draw her a *picture* of what she would look like with a shaved head. It IS Christmas, after all.

Thanks,
Tiki

DEAR SANTA,

Could you bring me a spiked collar? This family just doesn't GET me.

Sincerely,
Drusilla (formerly Fluffy)

Dear Santa,

Before jumping down our chimney this Christmas, could you please grab the bird bath that was accidentally left in the backyard? It actually belongs in the living room.

I'm sure it's heavy, but I figure since you lug giant bags of presents to all the cats in the world you are the best candidate for the job. Before you leave, could you also crack open the window? You're the best!

Your friend,
Charlie

DEAR SANTA,

I'm feeling extra charitable this Christmas. Enclosed are seven of my nine lives—please give them to another cat.

I guess I just feel so GREEDY keeping nine, you know? But that whole "knocking the armoire over" incident from last week was enough to convince me I should probably keep one extra life in the pipeline, just in case.

Thanks,
Tom

DEAR SANTA,

Thanks so much again for unknowingly signing up for my class, Yuletide Fat Blasting.

When you get here we'll warm up on the floor by stretching all the way out to expose the full length of our magnificent bellies. Then we'll leap up toward an invisible bug just out of reach on the wall. From there we'll move into some rebound flips off the same wall. We'll finish up the class with ten to twenty frantic sprints from one end of the house to the other.

You'll probably want to wear something a bit more breathable than velvet. A towel and shoes with strong arch support are also musts. And I'll obviously replace your cookies and milk with rice cakes and coconut water.

Get ready to feel the burn, Santa!

Love,
Gilly

DEAR SANTA,

The red dot KEEPS COMING BACK. This is really getting out of hand.

If my humans have mouse and bug traps, why not splurge on some red dot traps? I guess I'll have to ask for them.

Love,
Beetlejuice

Hi Santa,

This is sort of an embarrassing request:

There's a bag of cat treats there on the mantel. Could you give me some?

But instead of just tossing the treats on the floor, willy-nilly, can you please place exactly ten treats on alternating floorboards? The trail should lead from the living room to the kitchen. The last treat should be placed in the tenth row of kitchen tiles, on the tenth tile from the left of the counter.

Think of it as a metaphor: You're laying the foundation for a pleasant, orderly Christmas!

Oh, and don't kill me, but there are some latex gloves next to the treats . . .

Cindy

DEAR SANTA,

Can you bring me a big pile of dough this Christmas?*

Everyone in the house agrees I am an expert kneader, so I would like to assist in the holiday baking. Some of the cookies might have cat hair in them, but 'tis the season, am I right?

Sincerely,
Cassie

* The baking kind; but I wouldn't turn my nose up at cash!

DEAR SANTA,

Just between the two of us: The farts aren't always the dog's.

Since I'm not completely heartless and am feeling a bit guilty, please bring him some really great Christmas presents this year.

Your friend,
Ricky

DEAR SANTA,

Please refer to the attached JPEG.

This poster isn't inspiring—it's terrifying! He's hanging onto that branch by a single claw, for Pete's sake!

For Christmas, please bring my human a less cruel motivational poster for her office, one *not* featuring a poor kitty falling to his demise. That "cats always land feet first" thing is a load of bunk (I speak from experience).

Thank you,
Moe

DEAR SANTA,

Have you ever tried the water in the Christmas tree stand? It's out of this world! I'm not sure why no one has thought to market it, but as a born entrepreneur, I know a million-dollar idea when I taste one.

If you could assist me in sending some samples to a bottling plant, I promise to give you company stock options.

Your friend,
Susan

DEAR SANTA,

All I want for Christmas is five hours of uninterrupted napping. Six, max. Definitely no more than fifteen.

Sincerely,
Greta

Hi Santa,

Here I am! Up here, Santa!

Shh, please don't blow my cover. I get a pass for sleeping on top of the fridge, but I don't think my humans would be as tolerant of my sleeping at the top of the Christmas tree.

Tortie

DEAR SANTA,

I don't want much this Christmas, just a random collection of objects placed on the coffee table. Phone chargers and earrings are nice, but I won't turn my nose up at coins, bottle caps, and twisty ties.

Something filled with liquid and easily breakable would really be a coup, but I don't want to get too greedy.

Best,
Calvin

DEAR SANTA,

How do I know you're real? I'm having trouble wrapping my head around your existence, so I'll make a deal with you: Let me climb your beard. If it's fake, it will come off right away.

And if it's real, the yelling will be all the proof I'll require. Don't worry, I have amazing grip from practicing on the curtains!

Love,
Goofy

Hi Santa,

I would be beyond grateful if you hid the mistletoe.
All of these kitty kisses are really drying out my
tongue!

Ruth

Dear Santa,

Can you please bring my human some new hair ties?

I don't know why she was so peeved when she found my stash of them under the couch (they're fun to bat around—so sue me) and why she wanted to throw them away. If she blows the lint and fur off them, they are still perfectly useful!

Sincerely,
Jasmine

Dear Santa,

It's not like I ASKED to be hairless. But you should hear all the rude remarks I get from strangers. Some people are beyond tacky.

What is the full-body wig situation like for cats? Something in a nice calico pattern would be chic, or maybe a gleaming black-and-white tuxedo so I'm always dressed to impress.

Your friend,
Dominique

Dear Santa,

Eating all of that shiny ribbon was a huge mistake.
Do they make Tums for cats?

Best,
Leo

Dear Santa,

It is definitely NOT "just feet" at the end of the bed. I don't care what my humans say, and I don't understand all of their yelping when I'm only trying to protect them by pouncing on whatever terrible monsters are lurking beneath the bedspread.

Anyway, a see-through bedspread would end this debate once and for all.

Thanks,
Ginger

Dear Santa,

In an effort to better myself and my human next year, this Christmas I would love subscriptions to *The New Yorker* and *The Economist*.

I would list for you the "publications" I am currently forced to lie on, but I'm much too embarrassed to write their names.

Sprawling across these brainier magazines will raise my IQ. As a bonus, I can remain stretched out on them undisturbed, since my human will only put the new magazines out to appear smarter when company comes over, but secretly she'll keep reading the trashy ones.

Thank you,
John Brown

DEAR SANTA,

For Christmas this year I would like qwsdfjklnmm mmmmmmmmmmmm,,,,.....................

Oh, *very funny*, human. Sorry about that, Santa. Some people around here are obviously still bitter about my walking across the keyboard while she "finishes her dissertation," whatever THAT means.

For the record, I was doing her a favor. She needed a break, and I needed some love.

Sincerely,
Cricket

DEAR SANTA,

I feel you.

People think that it's okay to point and make rude comments about my "jiggly belly," too. They don't seem to care about my lifelong struggle with body image or consider that calling me "fatty" completely trivializes my very real thyroid problem.

I am always here if you need to vent.

Your friend,
Meatball

DEAR SANTA,

Assuming the package I mailed out a few months ago reached you safely, I can't wait to see what you and the elves have done with it.

Twenty pounds of cat hair should net us plenty of beautiful scarves, blankets, ponchos, etc. It's going to be a very merry, eco-friendly Christmas this year!

I'm always happy to do my part for the environment.

Your friend,
Gus

DEAR SANTA,

It's me, your pal Pancakes. Hi again!

It occurred to me after my last letter that I completely forgot about yogurt. Isn't yogurt the best? It's so good for you, and such a wonderful way to start your day off right.

Just brainstorming here: What if this Christmas we teamed up and you ate several weeks' worth of yogurt and left the container lids for *me*? Seems pretty win-win—you get healthy breakfasts, and I get a collection of hockey pucks to bat under the fridge. Teamwork!

Sincerely,
Pancakes

DEAR SANTA,

Gosh, I've just been so itchy lately—and congested and wheezy and teary-eyed . . .

You don't think I'm allergic to the new PUPPY, do you? That can't be it, right? Do you really think?

Oh, what a bummer. What a *total* bummer. I guess you'll just have to give him to another family as a Christmas gift.

As luck would have it, I found a large box with some holes in the lid and thick red ribbon in the office the other day. Would these maybe be useful? I've put them right under the Christmas tree for your convenience.

Sincerely,
Pete

DEAR SANTA,

I don't want any presents this Christmas. Seeing all of my humans and extended humans together, laughing and opening presents, is the greatest gift of all.

Ha! Just messing with you—of course I want the most presents out of everyone. I'll be counting.

Love,
Spook

DEAR SANTA,

Can you believe that there are people in this world who *don't* like cats? People who think they have seen *too many* cats, and cat products and cat paraphernalia? People who use the Internet to look at things *other than* pictures and videos of cats?

Nope, I've never met any of these people either—I was just checking.

Merry Christmas!

Love,
Scout